THE COMPLETE
VITAMIX BLENDER
COOKBOOK 2023

TRANSFORM YOUR HEALTH WITH 500 SMOOTHIES, SOUPS, SIDE DISHES, NUT BUTTERS, ICE CREAM, APPETIZERS, COOKIES, CAKES AND BAKING, ENTREES, BREADS, BABY FOOD

WELLNESS WRITINGS

Copyright © 2023

Table of Contents

INTRODUCTION

Welcome to "The Complete Vitamix Blender Cookbook 2023: Transform Your Health With 500 Smoothies, Soups, Side Dishes, Nut Butters, Ice Cream, Appetizers, Cookies, Cakes And Baking, Entrees, Breads, Baby Food" – A culinary adventure that will revolutionize your kitchen and elevate your cooking to new heights! Whether you're a seasoned home chef or a beginner in the world of cooking, this book is designed to be your ultimate guide to unleashing the full potential of your Vitamix blender.

Inside these pages, you'll discover a treasure trove of wholesome and mouthwatering recipes that cater to every taste and occasion. From hearty breakfasts to delectable desserts, refreshing smoothies to nourishing baby food, we've covered it all. But this cookbook offers so much more than just recipes.

Beyond the delicious dishes, you'll find expert tips, creative techniques, and insightful guidance that will empower you to create culinary masterpieces like never before. Our journey together goes beyond the kitchen – it's about discovering the art of blending flavors, creating unforgettable memories, and embracing the joy of cooking.

Each recipe has been carefully crafted to showcase the versatility of your Vitamix blender, making meal preparation a breeze. But what truly sets this book apart is the emphasis on nutritious and wholesome ingredients that will fuel your body with goodness.

As you embark on this culinary adventure, you'll find that cooking with the Vitamix blender is more than just a time-saving tool; it's a lifestyle choice that promotes health and wellness for you and your loved ones. From nutrient-packed smoothies that invigorate your mornings to sumptuous soups that warm your soul, every recipe has been thoughtfully curated to nourish your body and mind.

But the magic doesn't stop there. Our cookbook is also filled with heartwarming stories and personal experiences shared by fellow home cooks who have transformed their lives and cooking habits with the help of their Vitamix blenders. These inspiring anecdotes will motivate you to embrace your blender and experiment fearlessly in the kitchen.

So, if you're ready to embark on a culinary journey that will transform the way you cook, eat, and live, "The Complete Vitamix Blender Cookbook 2023" is your trusted companion. Get ready to create delightful dishes that will leave your family and friends amazed and your taste buds dancing with joy.

Let this book be your guide to blending health, happiness, and creativity into your everyday meals. Together, let's unlock the true potential of your Vitamix blender and make cooking a truly rewarding experience! Get your aprons on and your blenders ready – it's time to blend a world of flavors, nourishment, and culinary bliss right in your own kitchen. **Happy blending!**

WHAT IS A VITAMIX BLENDER

Vitamix is a blender on steroids. A regular blender does just what the name implies: blends. This product manages to cook *while* it blends, and quickly, too. Cooking a soup takes five minutes: throw the vegetables, broth and ingredients in and let the machine work its magic.

There are a few things that set these awesome machines apart:

- **It's Healthy.** Despite the fast cook times, fruits' and vegetables' nutritional values aren't lost, making Vitamix preferable to a microwave.
- **Speed.** Cook times are fast.
- **Quality.** I'm an avid crock-potting, soup-loving fiend, yet all my recipes have passed the taste test in my Vitamix.
- **Variety.** It makes cold smoothies are made as reliably as it does blended nut milk recipes.

Vitamix is a machine built around convenience. Its incredible processing speeds make complicated recipes, even hot soup recipes, in a matter of minutes. If you can afford to cut your cook times down to small fractions of the original, do something nice for your kitchen (and yourself) and splurge.

IS VITAMIX WORTH IT?

That's the exact question I asked myself before buying a Vitamix. Despite being a yes or no question, you need to know a lot more factors before you can make a thorough decision.

Luckily, I've covered all the variables on what makes Vitamix worth it in this article.

So, without further delay, let's find out if you should invest in a Vitamix blender.

Changing to a healthy lifestyle will be a lot easier

The most straightforward healthy food/drink I can think of is **smoothies,** depending on the ingredients. You can technically buy smoothies, but chances are it will have a ludicrous amount of sugar which is definitely not healthy. So, with a Vitamix, you can make healthy recipes—particularly smoothies—with no added sugars, no preservatives, nor chemical additives. Oh, and don't worry, your smoothies will still be sweet from fruits' natural sugar (if you choose to add sweet fruits, of course).

The other best example is canned soups, which could be unnecessarily high in sodium, contain preservatives, etc.

With a Vitamix, making healthy **hot soup** is just as easy as making a smoothie. As I have mentioned before, a Vitamix blender is so powerful that it can heat soup with just the blades' friction. So, all you need to do is add all the ingredients to the blender and blend for about 6 minutes at max speed.

Here's more:

Being healthy certainly doesn't mean to abstain from desserts. Basically, you can make a healthy version of ice cream called **nice cream** with Vitamix. Best of all? It's amazingly delicious even without adding any sugar!

And of course, Vitamix can make several healthy recipes, not just these three.

The point is:

When you make your own healthy food, you can customize what goes in. You can add more protein, less salt, add natural sweeteners, etc. This is precisely why a Vitamix blender can help you change to a healthier lifestyle.

Personal anecdote: Getting a Vitamix has turned me into a smoothie person. Technically, (pre-Vitamix) I bought smoothies from time to time, but I never made it daily since it's rather expensive. But, once I have my own powerful blender, smoothies have become a daily thing—as a breakfast, snack, or maybe even as a dinner!

It comes with a tamper:

Here's the thing, tamper is a solution for these problems: Air pockets are inevitable. So, with the help of a tamper, you can push back the ingredients to the blades.

Second, there are times (thick recipes) where constituents will get stuck on the sides. And with the same solution, you can use the tamper to push the components toward the blades.

Please note, air pockets are **NOT** *cavitation. I'll talk more about cavitation as we proceed.*

Here's the deal:

Blendtec made an attack ad against Vitamix's tamper—which actually ended up being comically ironic.

You see, it turns out that their regular pitchers can't handle thick blends properly. Essentially, you have to stop the operation, scrape the contents toward the blade, and blend over and over again. So, making nut butter will take more time and effort.

As a result, they made a separate container, particularly for thick blends.

Now, let's see why Vitamix's tamper is superior.

First and foremost, you don't need a different container for a thick recipe which will save you money. Secondly, you can use the tamper while operating since it's designed to not hit the blades when you use it through the opening lid. So, it's more effortless than having to do the "stop, scrape, blend, stop, scrape, blend."

Therefore, the use of a tamper will undoubtedly make your blending experience easier and faster.

It's super easy to clean

Just like its controls, cleanup is so straightforward. For starters, the newer series are dishwasher safe.

In fact, even without using the dishwasher, cleaning the blender is incredibly easy. Clearly, straightforward maintenance adds up to the question, is Vitamix worth it?

Anyway, here's how you clean the blender in 3 easy steps:

1. Add warm water to about half of the pitcher and add a little bit of dishwashing liquid. You can also rinse it before adding the soapy water.
2. Blend for 30 seconds at speed 7 or max (based on experience, using speed 7 is more than enough for cleaning).
3. After blending, rinse the pitcher and the lid and let dry.

This whole process will not even take you a minute, which is faster than using the dishwasher.

Moreover, this is what they mean by self-cleaning. You can clean the pitcher by using the blender's power itself. Also, some models highlight an auto-clean preset.

For the motor base, you only need to wipe it with a damp cloth. If you choose the **smart ascent series**, it features a touchscreen, so it's easier to wipe than the older models.

Available Accessories

Vitamix offers several accessories and attachments. Here are my favorites:

1. **Blending bowl** for dressings;
2. **Vitamix blending cup** for single-serve smoothies with double insulation to keep your drinks cold; and
3. **Vitamix food processor attachment** for slicing and shredding.

Of course, other attachments are handy. For instance, you should consider the dry grains container if you like to grind fresh flour for baking.

If you're more of a hot soup person, then a **stainless steel pitcher** is an excellent addition to your kitchen arsenal. There's also the so-called **Aer disc container** which is perfect for emulsifying drinks.

Furthermore, Vitamix also offers a **48-ounce vessel** if you only need small servings.

You can also get beneficial accessories such as the **under-blade scraper** and **tamper holder**.

Last but not least, Vitamix also offers a **smart scale** which brings me to my next point…

BREAKFAST AND BRUNCH RECIPES

Green Smoothie Bowl

Ingredients:
- 1 cup spinach leaves
- 1 frozen banana
- 1/2 cup frozen mango chunks
- 1/2 cup coconut water
- 1 tablespoon chia seeds
- Toppings: sliced strawberries, shredded coconut, granola

Instructions:
1. In your Vitamix blender, combine spinach, frozen banana, frozen mango, and coconut water.
2. Blend on high until smooth and creamy.
3. Pour the smoothie into a bowl and top with sliced strawberries, shredded coconut, and granola.
4. Enjoy this nutritious and delicious green smoothie bowl for a refreshing breakfast or brunch.

Calories: 277 Protein: 40g Carbohydrates: 5g
Dietary Fiber: 5g Sugars: 8g Fat: 8g

Blueberry Almond Pancakes

Ingredients:
- 1 cup all-purpose flour
- 1 tablespoon sugar
- 1 teaspoon baking powder
- 1/2 teaspoon baking soda
- 1/4 teaspoon salt
- 1 cup almond milk
- 1 large egg
- 1 tablespoon vegetable oil
- 1/2 cup fresh blueberries

Instructions:
1. In a mixing bowl, whisk together flour, sugar, baking powder, baking soda, and salt.
2. In a separate bowl, whisk together almond milk, egg, and vegetable oil.
3. Pour the wet ingredients into the dry ingredients and stir until just combined.
4. Gently fold in the fresh blueberries.
5. Preheat a griddle or non-stick skillet over medium heat and lightly grease with cooking spray.
6. Pour 1/4 cup of the pancake batter onto the griddle for each pancake.
7. Cook until bubbles form on the surface, then flip and cook until golden brown on the other side.

8. Serve these fluffy and flavorful blueberry almond pancakes with maple syrup or your favorite toppings.

Calories:450 Protein: 3g Carbohydrates: 15g
Dietary Fiber: 2g Sugars: 4g Fat: 7g

Avocado Toast with Poached Eggs

Ingredients:
- 2 slices whole-grain bread
- 1 ripe avocado, peeled and pitted
- 1 tablespoon lemon juice
- Salt and pepper to taste
- 2 large eggs
- 1 teaspoon white vinegar
- Optional toppings: red pepper flakes, sliced radishes, microgreens

Instructions:
1. Toast the whole-grain bread slices until crispy.
2. In a bowl, mash the ripe avocado with lemon juice, salt, and pepper until smooth.
3. Poach the eggs: Fill a saucepan with water and add white vinegar. Bring to a simmer.

4. Carefully crack the eggs into the simmering water and cook for 3-4 minutes until the whites are set but the yolks are still runny.
5. Remove the poached eggs with a slotted spoon and drain on a paper towel.
6. Spread the avocado mixture on the toasted bread slices.
7. Top each toast with a poached egg and sprinkle with optional toppings, such as red pepper flakes, sliced radishes, or microgreens.
8. Enjoy this nutritious and satisfying avocado toast with poached eggs for a delightful breakfast or brunch option.

Calories: 350 Protein: 30g Carbohydrates: 25g
Dietary Fiber: 10g Sugars: 3g Fat: 20g

Tropical Mango Smoothie

Ingredients:
- 1 ripe mango, peeled and pitted
- 1/2 cup pineapple chunks
- 1/2 cup coconut milk
- 1 tablespoon honey or maple syrup
- 1/2 cup ice cubes

Instructions:
1. In your Vitamix blender, add the ripe mango, pineapple chunks, coconut milk, honey or maple syrup, and ice cubes.
2. Blend on high until smooth and creamy.
3. Pour the tropical mango smoothie into a glass and garnish with a slice of fresh mango or a sprinkle of shredded coconut.
4. Sip on this refreshing and tropical smoothie for a boost of energy and a taste of paradise.

Calories: 250 Protein: 10g Carbohydrates: 45g
Dietary Fiber: 5g Sugars: 40g Fat: 8g

Spinach and Feta Egg Cups

Ingredients:
- 6 large eggs
- 1/4 cup milk
- 1 cup fresh spinach, chopped
- 1/2 cup crumbled feta cheese
- Salt and pepper to taste
- Cooking spray

Instructions:
1. Preheat your oven to 350°F (175°C) and lightly grease a muffin tin with cooking spray.
2. In a mixing bowl, whisk together the eggs and milk until well combined.
3. Stir in the chopped spinach and crumbled feta cheese. Season with salt and pepper to taste.
4. Pour the egg mixture evenly into the muffin tin cups.
5. Bake in the preheated oven for about 15-20 minutes or until the egg cups are set and slightly golden on top.
6. Remove the egg cups from the oven and let them cool slightly before serving.
7. These spinach and feta egg cups are a convenient and protein-packed breakfast or brunch option that can be made ahead of time and enjoyed on the go.

Calories: 350 Protein: 40g Carbohydrates: 35g
Dietary Fiber: 10g Sugars: 3g Fat: 20g

Creamy Oatmeal with Berries

Ingredients:
- 1 cup rolled oats
- 2 cups almond milk
- 1 tablespoon honey or maple syrup
- 1/2 teaspoon vanilla extract
- Fresh berries for topping

Instructions:
1. In a saucepan, combine the rolled oats and almond milk. Bring to a boil over medium heat.
2. Reduce the heat to low and simmer, stirring occasionally, until the oats are cooked and the mixture thickens, about 5-7 minutes.
3. Stir in the honey or maple syrup and vanilla extract.
4. Remove the creamy oatmeal from the heat and let it cool slightly.
5. Serve the oatmeal in bowls and top with fresh berries for a delicious and nutritious breakfast to start your day right.

Calories: 250 Protein: 30g Carbohydrates: 45g
Dietary Fiber: 5g Sugars: 8g Fat: 8g

Cinnamon Apple Pancakes

Ingredients:
- 1 cup all-purpose flour
- 1 tablespoon sugar
- 1 teaspoon baking powder
- 1/2 teaspoon baking soda
- 1/4 teaspoon salt
- 1 cup buttermilk
- 1 large egg
- 2 tablespoons melted butter
- 1 teaspoon ground cinnamon
- 1 apple, peeled, cored, and thinly sliced

Instructions:
1. In a mixing bowl, whisk together the flour, sugar, baking powder, baking soda, and salt.
2. In a separate bowl, whisk together the buttermilk, egg, melted butter, and ground cinnamon.
3. Pour the wet ingredients into the dry ingredients and stir until just combined.
4. Gently fold in the thinly sliced apple.
5. Preheat a griddle or non-stick skillet over medium heat and lightly grease with cooking spray.

6. Pour 1/4 cup of the pancake batter onto the griddle for each pancake.
7. Cook until bubbles form on the surface, then flip and cook until golden brown on the other side.
8. Serve these scrumptious cinnamon apple pancakes with a drizzle of maple syrup for a delightful breakfast treat.

Calories: 200 Protein: 3g Carbohydrates: 35g Dietary Fiber: 3g Sugars: 5g Fat: 3g Saturated Fat: 1.5g

Avocado and Spinach Green Smoothie

Ingredients:
- 1 ripe avocado, peeled and pitted
- 1 cup fresh spinach leaves
- 1/2 cup cucumber, chopped
- 1/2 banana
- 1 tablespoon chia seeds
- 1 cup almond milk
- 1 tablespoon honey or agave syrup (optional for added sweetness)
- Ice cubes

Instructions:
1. In your Vitamix blender, add the ripe avocado, fresh spinach leaves, chopped cucumber, banana, chia seeds, almond milk, and honey or agave syrup (if using).
2. Blend on high until the smoothie is creamy and well combined.
3. Add ice cubes and blend again until you reach your desired consistency.
4. Pour the avocado and spinach green smoothie into a glass and enjoy a nutrient-packed and refreshing way to kickstart your day.

Calories: 300 Protein: 10g Carbohydrates: 25g
Dietary Fiber: 10g Sugars: 15g Fat: 20g

Lemon Poppy Seed Muffins

Ingredients:
- 1 1/2 cups all-purpose flour
- 1/2 cup sugar
- 2 teaspoons baking powder
- 1/4 teaspoon baking soda
- 1/4 teaspoon salt
- 1/4 cup unsalted butter, melted

- 1/2 cup milk
- 1/4 cup fresh lemon juice
- 1 tablespoon lemon zest
- 1 large egg
- 1 tablespoon poppy seeds

Instructions:
1. Preheat your oven to 375°F (190°C) and line a muffin tin with paper liners.
2. In a large mixing bowl, whisk together the flour, sugar, baking powder, baking soda, and salt.
3. In a separate bowl, whisk together the melted butter, milk, fresh lemon juice, lemon zest, and egg.
4. Pour the wet ingredients into the dry ingredients and stir until just combined.
5. Gently fold in the poppy seeds.
6. Divide the batter evenly among the muffin cups, filling each about 3/4 full.
7. Bake in the preheated oven for about 15-18 minutes or until a toothpick inserted into the center of a muffin comes out clean.
8. Let the lemon poppy seed muffins cool in the tin for a few minutes before transferring them to a wire rack to cool completely.
9. These zesty and delightful muffins make for a wonderful breakfast or brunch option.

Calories: 250 Protein: 3g Carbohydrates: 35g
Dietary Fiber: 1g Sugars: 15g Fat: 13g

Quinoa Breakfast Bowl

Ingredients:
- 1 cup cooked quinoa
- 1/2 cup Greek yogurt
- 1/4 cup fresh berries (strawberries, blueberries, or raspberries)
- 1 tablespoon honey or maple syrup
- 1 tablespoon almond butter or peanut butter
- 1 tablespoon chia seeds
- A sprinkle of cinnamon

Instructions:
1. In a serving bowl, layer the cooked quinoa and Greek yogurt.
2. Top with fresh berries, drizzle with honey or maple syrup, and add a dollop of almond butter or peanut butter.
3. Sprinkle chia seeds and cinnamon over the top for added texture and flavor.
4. Mix everything together and enjoy a satisfying and protein-rich quinoa breakfast bowl that will keep you fueled throughout the day.

Calories: 250 Protein: 10g Carbohydrates: 45g
Dietary Fiber: 5g Sugars: 8g Fat: 4g

Spinach and Feta Omelette

Ingredients:
- 3 large eggs
- 1 cup fresh spinach leaves
- 1/4 cup crumbled feta cheese
- 1/4 cup diced tomatoes
- Salt and pepper to taste
- 1 tablespoon olive oil

Instructions:
1. In a bowl, whisk the eggs until well beaten, and season with salt and pepper.
2. Heat the olive oil in a non-stick skillet over medium heat.
3. Add the whisked eggs to the skillet and cook for a few minutes until the edges start to set.
4. Sprinkle the fresh spinach leaves, crumbled feta cheese, and diced tomatoes over one-half of the omelette.
5. Fold the other half of the omelette over the filling and cook for another minute or until the cheese melts.
6. Slide the omelette onto a plate and serve hot with a side of toast or fresh fruit.

Calories: 250 Protein: 20g Carbohydrates: 15g
Dietary Fiber: 4g Sugars: 2g Fat: 5g

As we round up this chapter, we humbly request your help in two ways:

1. Share Your Feedback: If you've enjoyed this chapter and its delicious recipes, we would be grateful for your honest positive review.

2. Stay in Touch: To make sure you don't miss out on future exciting cookbooks and culinary creations, please consider following our Amazon Author Page. This way, you'll be among the first to know about our latest releases, special offers, and culinary inspirations.

Creamy Hummus:

Ingredients:
- 1 can (15 oz) chickpeas, drained and rinsed
- 1/4 cup tahini
- 1/4 cup lemon juice
- 2 cloves garlic
- 2 tablespoons olive oil
- 1/2 teaspoon ground cumin
- Salt and pepper to taste

Instructions:
1. Place all the ingredients in the Vitamix blender.
2. Blend on high speed until smooth and creamy.
3. Adjust seasonings to taste.
4. Serve with pita bread, fresh vegetables, or as a spread on sandwiches.

Calories: 80g Protein: 3g Carbohydrates: 7g Dietary Fiber: 3g Sugars: 2g Fat: 7g Saturated Fat: 1.5g

Guacamole

Ingredients:
- 2 ripe avocados, peeled and pitted
- 1 small onion, chopped
- 1 ripe tomato, diced
- 1 jalapeno, seeded and chopped
- 1/4 cup fresh cilantro
- 2 tablespoons lime juice
- Salt and pepper to taste

Instructions:
1. Add avocados, onion, tomato, jalapeno, cilantro, and lime juice to the Vitamix blender.
2. Blend on low speed until ingredients are combined but still chunky.
3. Season with salt and pepper to taste.
4. Serve with tortilla chips or as a topping for tacos and salads.

Calories: 50 Protein: 3g Carbohydrates: 5g Dietary Fiber: 3g Sugars: 2g Fat: 4g Saturated Fat: 1.5g

Spinach Artichoke Dip

Ingredients:
- 1 cup cooked spinach, drained and chopped
- 1 cup canned artichoke hearts, drained
- 1/2 cup sour cream
- 1/2 cup mayonnaise
- 1 cup shredded mozzarella cheese
- 1/4 cup grated Parmesan cheese
- 2 cloves garlic
- Salt and pepper to taste

Instructions:
1. Place cooked spinach, artichoke hearts, sour cream, mayonnaise, mozzarella cheese, Parmesan cheese, and garlic in the Vitamix blender.
2. Blend on low speed until well combined.
3. Season with salt and pepper to taste.
4. Transfer the mixture to a baking dish and bake in the oven at 350°F (175°C) for about 20 minutes, or until bubbly and golden brown.
5. Serve with tortilla chips or sliced baguette.

Calories: 250 Protein: 6g Carbohydrates: 7g Dietary Fiber: 2g Sugars: 2g Fat: 20g

Fresh Tomato Salsa

Ingredients:
- 4 ripe tomatoes, diced
- 1/2 onion, chopped
- 1 jalapeno, seeded and chopped
- 1/4 cup fresh cilantro
- 2 tablespoons lime juice
- Salt and pepper to taste

Instructions:
1. Add diced tomatoes, chopped onion, jalapeno, cilantro, and lime juice to the Vitamix blender.
2. Pulse on low speed until ingredients are combined but still chunky.
3. Season with salt and pepper to taste.
4. Serve with tortilla chips or as a topping for grilled chicken or fish.

Calories: 20 Protein: 2g Carbohydrates: 5g Dietary Fiber: 2g Sugars: 3g Fat: 8g

Sweet Potato Fries

Ingredients:
- 2 large sweet potatoes, peeled and cut into fries
- 2 tablespoons olive oil
- 1 teaspoon paprika
- 1/2 teaspoon garlic powder
- Salt and pepper to taste

Instructions:
1. Preheat the oven to 425°F (220°C) and line a baking sheet with parchment paper.
2. Toss the sweet potato fries with olive oil, paprika, garlic powder, salt, and pepper in a large bowl.
3. Arrange the fries in a single layer on the prepared baking sheet.
4. Bake for 20-25 minutes, flipping halfway through, or until the fries are crispy and golden brown.
5. Serve as a tasty and healthy snack.

Calories: 150 Protein: 2g Carbohydrates: 25g
Dietary Fiber: 4g Sugars: 5g Fat: 5g

Roasted Red Pepper Hummus:

Ingredients:
- 1 can (15 oz) chickpeas, drained and rinsed
- 1 cup roasted red peppers (from a jar)
- 1/4 cup tahini
- 2 cloves garlic
- 2 tablespoons lemon juice
- 2 tablespoons olive oil
- 1/2 teaspoon ground cumin
- Salt and pepper to taste

Instructions:
1. Combine chickpeas, roasted red peppers, tahini, garlic, lemon juice, olive oil, cumin, salt, and pepper in the Vitamix blender.
2. Blend on high speed until smooth and creamy.
3. Adjust seasonings to taste.
4. Serve with pita bread, vegetable sticks, or use as a spread in wraps and sandwiches.

Calories: 80g Protein: 4g Carbohydrates: 10g
Dietary Fiber: 3g Sugars: 2g Fat: 8g

Creamy Avocado Dip:

Ingredients:
- 2 ripe avocados, peeled and pitted
- 1/4 cup Greek yogurt
- 1/4 cup fresh cilantro
- 2 cloves garlic
- 1 jalapeno, seeded
- 2 tablespoons lime juice
- Salt and pepper to taste

Instructions:
1. Place avocados, Greek yogurt, cilantro, garlic, jalapeno, lime juice, salt, and pepper in the Vitamix blender.
2. Blend on low speed until the mixture is smooth and creamy.
3. Season with additional salt and pepper if desired.
4. Serve with tortilla chips, vegetable crudités, or as a topping for tacos and grilled meats.

Calories:100 Protein: 3g Carbohydrates: 5g Dietary Fiber: 4g Sugars: 2g Fat:7g

Cheesy Cauliflower Bites:

Ingredients:
- 1 medium head cauliflower, cut into florets
- 1 cup shredded cheddar cheese
- 1/4 cup grated Parmesan cheese
- 2 eggs
- 1/2 teaspoon garlic powder
- 1/2 teaspoon onion powder
- Salt and pepper to taste

Instructions:
1. Preheat the oven to 400°F (200°C) and line a baking sheet with parchment paper.
2. Steam the cauliflower florets until tender, then let them cool slightly.
3. In the Vitamix blender, combine the steamed cauliflower, cheddar cheese, Parmesan cheese, eggs, garlic powder, onion powder, salt, and pepper.
4. Blend on low speed until the mixture is well combined.
5. Scoop tablespoon-sized portions of the mixture onto the prepared baking sheet and flatten slightly with the back of a spoon.
6. Bake for 15-20 minutes or until the bites are golden and crispy.
7. Serve as a delightful and cheesy finger food.

Calories: 250 Protein: 15g Carbohydrates: 15g
Dietary Fiber: 3g Sugars: 4g Fat: 14g

Fresh Basil Pesto

Ingredients:
- 2 cups fresh basil leaves
- 1/2 cup grated Parmesan cheese
- 1/3 cup pine nuts or walnuts
- 2 cloves garlic
- 1/2 cup olive oil
- Salt and pepper to taste

Instructions:
1. In the Vitamix blender, add basil leaves, Parmesan cheese, pine nuts or walnuts, and garlic.
2. Blend on low speed while gradually adding the olive oil until the pesto reaches the desired consistency.
3. Season with salt and pepper to taste.
4. Use as a pasta sauce, spread on bruschetta, or as a flavor boost to your favorite dishes.

Calories: 200 Protein: 3g Carbohydrates: 2g Dietary Fiber: 1g Sugars: 0g Fat: 20g

Beetroot Hummus:

Ingredients:
- 1 can (15 oz) chickpeas, drained and rinsed
- 1 large cooked beetroot, peeled and chopped
- 1/4 cup tahini
- 2 cloves garlic
- 2 tablespoons lemon juice
- 2 tablespoons olive oil
- 1/2 teaspoon ground cumin
- Salt and pepper to taste

Instructions:
1. Combine chickpeas, cooked beetroot, tahini, garlic, lemon juice, olive oil, cumin, salt, and pepper in the Vitamix blender.
2. Blend on high speed until the hummus is smooth and creamy.
3. Adjust seasonings to taste.
4. Serve with pita chips, vegetable sticks, or use as a vibrant dip for various snacks.

Calories: 150 Protein: 3g Carbohydrates: 9g Dietary Fiber: 3g Sugars: 3g Fat: 8

Spicy Mango Salsa:

Ingredients:
- 2 ripe mangoes, peeled and diced
- 1/2 cup diced red onion
- 1 jalapeno, seeded and finely chopped
- 1/4 cup chopped fresh cilantro
- 2 tablespoons lime juice
- 1 tablespoon honey
- Salt and pepper to taste

Instructions:
1. In the Vitamix blender, add one diced mango, red onion, jalapeno, cilantro, lime juice, honey, salt, and pepper.
2. Pulse a few times until the mixture is well combined but still chunky.
3. Transfer the mixture to a bowl and stir in the remaining diced mango.
4. Chill in the refrigerator for at least 30 minutes before serving.
5. Serve as a zesty topping for grilled chicken, fish, or enjoy with tortilla chips.

Calories: 40g Protein: 1g Carbohydrates: 10g
Dietary Fiber: 2g Sugars: 7g Fat: 1g

Sun-Dried Tomato Pesto:

Ingredients:
- 1 cup sun-dried tomatoes (packed in oil), drained
- 1/2 cup fresh basil leaves
- 1/4 cup grated Parmesan cheese (or nutritional yeast for a dairy-free option)
- 2 cloves garlic
- 1/4 cup pine nuts (or walnuts)
- 1/4 cup olive oil
- Salt and pepper to taste

Instructions:
1. In the Vitamix blender, combine sun-dried tomatoes, basil leaves, Parmesan cheese, garlic, and pine nuts.
2. Blend on low speed until the ingredients are roughly chopped.
3. Slowly drizzle in the olive oil while continuing to blend until the pesto reaches a smooth consistency.
4. Season with salt and pepper to taste.
5. Toss with cooked pasta, spread on sandwiches, or use as a flavorful marinade for grilled chicken.

Calories: 80 Protein: 3g Carbohydrates:4g Dietary Fiber: 2g Sugars: 3g Fat: 5g

Zesty Cucumber Salsa:

Ingredients:
- 2 large cucumbers, diced
- 1 small red onion, finely chopped
- 1 jalapeno, seeded and diced
- 1/4 cup chopped fresh cilantro
- 2 tablespoons lime juice
- 1 tablespoon apple cider vinegar
- 1 tablespoon honey (or agave nectar for a vegan option)
- Salt and pepper to taste

Instructions:
1. In the Vitamix blender, pulse one diced cucumber to create a smooth base for the salsa.
2. In a bowl, combine the blended cucumber, remaining diced cucumber, red onion, jalapeno, cilantro, lime juice, apple cider vinegar, honey, salt, and pepper.
3. Mix well until all the flavors meld together.
4. Refrigerate for at least 30 minutes before serving.
5. Enjoy as a refreshing salsa with tortilla chips or as a topping for grilled fish.

Calories: 35 Protein: 1g Carbohydrates:7g Dietary Fiber: 2g Sugars: 4g Fat: 1g

SOUPS AND SALADS RECIPE

Creamy Roasted Tomato Soup:

Ingredients:
- 4 cups cherry tomatoes
- 1 small onion, quartered
- 3 garlic cloves
- 2 tablespoons olive oil
- 1 cup vegetable broth
- 1/2 cup coconut milk (or heavy cream for a non-vegan option)
- 1 teaspoon dried basil
- Salt and pepper to taste
- Fresh basil leaves, for garnish

Instructions:
1. Preheat the oven to 400°F (200°C). On a baking sheet, toss cherry tomatoes, onion, and garlic with olive oil, salt, and pepper.
2. Roast in the oven for 25-30 minutes until the tomatoes are soft and slightly charred.
3. In the Vitamix blender, combine the roasted tomatoes, onion, and garlic with vegetable broth, coconut milk, and dried basil.
4. Blend on high speed until the soup is smooth and creamy.
5. Transfer the soup to a saucepan and heat over medium heat until warmed through.

6. Season with additional salt and pepper if needed.
7. Serve hot with fresh basil leaves as a garnish.

Calories: 250 Protein: 30g Carbohydrates: 15g Dietary Fiber: 5g Sugars: 8g Fat: 8g Saturated Fat: 1.5g

Curried Carrot Soup

Ingredients:
- 4 cups carrots, chopped
- 1 small onion, chopped
- 2 tablespoons olive oil
- 1 tablespoon curry powder
- 4 cups vegetable broth
- 1 cup coconut milk (or almond milk for a lighter option)
- 1 tablespoon fresh ginger, grated
- Salt and pepper to taste
- Fresh cilantro, for garnish

Instructions:
1. In a large pot, sauté chopped carrots and onion in olive oil until slightly softened.
2. Add curry powder and cook for another minute to release its flavors.
3. Transfer the sautéed vegetables to the Vitamix blender, along with vegetable broth, coconut milk, and grated ginger.
4. Blend on high speed until the soup is smooth and creamy.
5. Pour the mixture back into the pot and heat over medium heat until warmed through.
6. Season with salt and pepper to taste.
7. Serve hot, garnished with fresh cilantro.

Calories: 250 Protein: 5g Carbohydrates: 20g Dietary Fiber: 5g Sugars: 8g Fat: 15g Saturated Fat: 1.5g

Creamy Avocado Gazpacho

Ingredients:
- 2 large tomatoes, diced
- 1 cucumber, peeled and diced
- 1 red bell pepper, diced
- 1/2 small red onion, diced
- 2 avocados, peeled and pitted
- 2 cups vegetable broth
- 1/4 cup fresh cilantro leaves
- 2 tablespoons lime juice
- Salt and pepper to taste
- Toasted pumpkin seeds, for garnish

Instructions:
1. In the Vitamix blender, combine diced tomatoes, cucumber, red bell pepper, red onion, avocados, vegetable broth, cilantro, and lime juice.
2. Blend on low speed until the gazpacho is slightly chunky and well combined.
3. Season with salt and pepper to taste.
4. Chill the gazpacho in the refrigerator for at least 30 minutes before serving.
5. Serve cold, garnished with toasted pumpkin seeds.

Calories: 200 Protein: 5g Carbohydrates: 12g Dietary Fiber: 5g Sugars: 8g Fat: 10g Saturated Fat: 1.5g

Strawberry Spinach Salad Dressing

Ingredients:
- 1 cup fresh strawberries, hulled and halved
- 2 tablespoons balsamic vinegar
- 2 tablespoons olive oil
- 1 tablespoon honey (or maple syrup for a vegan option)
- 1/4 teaspoon Dijon mustard
- Salt and pepper to taste

Instructions:
1. In the Vitamix blender, blend strawberries, balsamic vinegar, olive oil, honey, Dijon mustard, salt, and pepper until the dressing is smooth and well combined.
2. Adjust sweetness and tanginess to your preference.
3. Drizzle the dressing over a bed of fresh spinach and toss to coat.
4. Add sliced strawberries, nuts, and feta cheese (or a vegan alternative) to the salad for added texture and flavor.

Calories: 60g Protein: 1g Carbohydrates: 8g Dietary Fiber: 2g Sugars: 6g Fat: 8g Saturated Fat: 1.5g

Creamy Cucumber Dill Salad Dressing

Ingredients:
- 1 large cucumber, peeled and chopped
- 1/4 cup fresh dill
- 1/4 cup plain Greek yogurt (or dairy-free yogurt for a vegan option)
- 2 tablespoons lemon juice
- 2 tablespoons olive oil
- 1 garlic clove
- Salt and pepper to taste

Instructions:
1. In the Vitamix blender, combine chopped cucumber, dill, Greek yogurt, lemon juice, olive oil, garlic, salt, and pepper.
2. Blend on high speed until the dressing is smooth and creamy.
3. Taste and adjust seasonings as needed.
4. Use the dressing to top a refreshing cucumber salad or drizzle over mixed greens for a light and tangy twist.

Calories: 20g Protein: 2g Carbohydrates: 2g Dietary Fiber: 1g Sugars: 2g Fat: 8g Saturated Fat: 1.5g

Creamy Cauliflower Potato Soup

Ingredients:
- 1 small head of cauliflower, chopped
- 2 medium-sized potatoes, peeled and chopped
- 1 small onion, diced
- 2 garlic cloves, minced
- 4 cups vegetable broth
- 1 cup unsweetened almond milk (or any milk of your choice)
- 1 tablespoon olive oil
- Salt and pepper to taste
- Fresh chives, for garnish

Instructions:
1. In a large pot, sauté diced onion and minced garlic in olive oil until translucent.
2. Add chopped cauliflower and potatoes to the pot and cook for a few minutes until slightly softened.
3. Pour in the vegetable broth and bring to a boil. Reduce heat and simmer until the vegetables are tender.
4. Transfer the mixture to the Vitamix blender, add almond milk, and blend on high speed until smooth and creamy.

5. Pour the soup back into the pot and heat over medium heat until warmed through.
6. Season with salt and pepper to taste.
7. Serve hot, garnished with fresh chives.

Calories: 150 Protein: 5g Carbohydrates: 20g Dietary Fiber: 4g Sugars: 8g Fat: 10g Saturated Fat: 3g

Avocado Lime Dressing

Ingredients:
- 2 ripe avocados, peeled and pitted
- 1/4 cup fresh lime juice
- 1/4 cup olive oil
- 1 garlic clove
- 2 tablespoons fresh cilantro
- 1/4 cup water (adjust for desired consistency)
- Salt and pepper to taste

Instructions:
1. In the Vitamix blender, blend avocados, lime juice, olive oil, garlic, cilantro, and water until the dressing is creamy and well combined.

2. Add more water if a thinner consistency is preferred.
3. Season with salt and pepper to taste.
4. Drizzle the dressing over your favorite salads or use it as a dip for veggies.

Calories: 200 Protein: 8g Carbohydrates: 22g Dietary Fiber: 4g Sugars: 8g Fat: 10g Saturated Fat: 2g

Quinoa and Chickpea Salad:

Ingredients:
- 1 cup cooked quinoa
- 1 can (15 oz) chickpeas, drained and rinsed
- 1 cup cherry tomatoes, halved
- 1/2 cucumber, diced
- 1/4 cup red onion, finely chopped
- 1/4 cup fresh parsley, chopped
- 2 tablespoons fresh lemon juice
- 2 tablespoons olive oil
- Salt and pepper to taste

Instructions:
1. In a large bowl, combine cooked quinoa, chickpeas, cherry tomatoes, cucumber, red onion, and fresh parsley.
2. In a small bowl, whisk together fresh lemon juice, olive oil, salt, and pepper to make the dressing.
3. Pour the dressing over the quinoa mixture and toss until everything is evenly coated.
4. Serve the quinoa and chickpea salad as a refreshing and filling side dish.

Calories: 350 Protein: 10g Carbohydrates: 45g Dietary Fiber: 9g Sugars: 5g Fat: 12g Saturated Fat: 1.5g

Pesto Zucchini Noodles:

Ingredients:
- 4 medium zucchinis, spiralized into noodles
- 1 cup fresh basil leaves
- 1/4 cup pine nuts
- 1/4 cup grated Parmesan cheese (or nutritional yeast for a vegan option)
- 2 garlic cloves
- 1/4 cup olive oil
- Salt and pepper to taste

Instructions:
1. In the Vitamix blender, blend fresh basil leaves, pine nuts, grated Parmesan cheese, garlic, olive oil, salt, and pepper until the pesto is smooth and well combined.
2. In a large skillet, sauté the zucchini noodles in a drizzle of olive oil over medium heat until they are tender.
3. Toss the zucchini noodles with the prepared pesto until they are evenly coated.
4. Serve as a light and flavorful main course or side dish.

Calories: 250 Protein: 7g Carbohydrates: 5g Dietary Fiber: 3g Sugars: 4g Fat:22g Saturated Fat: 1.5g

Spicy Salsa Verde:

Ingredients:
- 4 tomatillos, husks removed and rinsed
- 1 jalapeño pepper, seeds removed for milder heat
- 1/2 onion, chopped
- 1/4 cup fresh cilantro
- 2 garlic cloves

- 1 tablespoon fresh lime juice
- Salt and pepper to taste

Instructions:
1. In the Vitamix blender, blend tomatillos, jalapeño pepper, chopped onion, fresh cilantro, garlic, fresh lime juice, salt, and pepper until the salsa is smooth and zesty.
2. Enjoy this flavorful salsa verde with tortilla chips, tacos, or as a condiment for your favorite dishes.

Calories: 20 Protein: 1g Carbohydrates: 2g Dietary Fiber: 2g Sugars: 2g Fat: 1g

Creamy Cauliflower Soup

Ingredients:
- 1 medium cauliflower head, chopped into florets
- 1/2 onion, chopped
- 2 garlic cloves
- 3 cups vegetable broth
- 1/2 cup heavy cream (or coconut cream for a dairy-free option)
- 2 tablespoons olive oil
- Salt and pepper to taste

Instructions:

1. In the Vitamix blender, blend chopped cauliflower florets, chopped onion, garlic, vegetable broth, heavy cream, olive oil, salt, and pepper until the soup is smooth and creamy.
2. Transfer the mixture to a pot and heat over medium heat until warmed through.
3. Serve this velvety cauliflower soup as a comforting appetizer or light lunch.

Calories: 70 Protein: 4g Carbohydrates: 6g Dietary Fiber: 2g Sugars: 3g Fat: 4g

VEGETABLE AND SIDES RECIPES

Creamy Cauliflower Mashed Potatoes:

Ingredients:
- 1 medium cauliflower head, chopped into florets
- 2 large russet potatoes, peeled and chopped
- 1/4 cup unsalted butter (or vegan butter for a dairy-free option)
- 1/4 cup milk (or almond milk for a dairy-free option)
- Salt and pepper to taste

Instructions:
1. In a large pot, boil the chopped cauliflower and potatoes until tender. Drain the water.
2. In the Vitamix blender, blend the cooked cauliflower and potatoes with unsalted butter, milk, salt, and pepper until smooth and creamy.
3. Serve these delicious cauliflower mashed potatoes as a healthier alternative to traditional mashed potatoes.

Calories: 150 Protein: 4g Carbohydrates: 25g
Dietary Fiber: 5g Sugars: 3g Fat: 7g

Sweet Potato Mash with Brown Butter:

Ingredients:
- 2 large sweet potatoes, peeled and chopped
- 4 tablespoons unsalted butter
- 1/4 cup milk (or almond milk for a dairy-free option)
- 1 tablespoon maple syrup
- 1/4 teaspoon ground cinnamon
- Salt and pepper to taste

Instructions:
1. In a pot, boil the chopped sweet potatoes until fork-tender. Drain the water.
2. In a small saucepan, melt the unsalted butter over medium heat, stirring continuously until it turns brown and gives off a nutty aroma. Be careful not to burn it.
3. In the Vitamix blender, blend the cooked sweet potatoes, brown butter, milk, maple syrup, ground cinnamon, salt, and pepper until smooth and creamy.
4. Serve this delectable sweet potato mash as a flavorful and comforting side dish.

Calories: 200 Protein: 3g Carbohydrates: 20g
Dietary Fiber: 4g Sugars: 8g Fat: 8g

Creamy Mushroom Risotto:

Ingredients:
- 1 cup Arborio rice
- 2 cups vegetable broth
- 1 cup sliced mushrooms
- 1/2 cup grated Parmesan cheese (or nutritional yeast for a dairy-free option)
- 2 tablespoons unsalted butter (or vegan butter)
- 1/4 cup white wine (optional)
- 1 garlic clove
- Salt and pepper to taste

Instructions:
1. In a pot, sauté the sliced mushrooms in unsalted butter until they release their moisture and turn golden brown. Add minced garlic and cook for another minute.
2. Add Arborio rice to the pot and toast for 1-2 minutes until lightly golden.
3. If using white wine, pour it into the pot and let it simmer until absorbed.
4. Gradually add vegetable broth, 1/2 cup at a time, stirring continuously until the rice is creamy and cooked al dente.
5. In the Vitamix blender, blend 1/2 cup of cooked mushrooms and vegetable broth until smooth.
6. Stir the blended mixture and grated Parmesan cheese into the risotto until well combined.

7. Serve this rich and creamy mushroom risotto as a comforting and satisfying side dish.

Calories: 250 Protein: 10g Carbohydrates: 45g Dietary Fiber: 4g Sugars: 4g Fat: 8g

Vegan Cashew Alfredo Sauce:

Ingredients:
- 1 cup raw cashews, soaked in water for at least 2 hours
- 1 cup vegetable broth
- 1/2 cup unsweetened almond milk
- 2 tablespoons nutritional yeast
- 1 tablespoon lemon juice
- 1 garlic clove
- Salt and pepper to taste

Instructions:
1. Drain the soaked cashews and add them to the Vitamix blender along with vegetable broth, almond milk, nutritional yeast, lemon juice, garlic, salt, and pepper.

2. Blend the mixture until the cashew Alfredo sauce is smooth and creamy.
3. Reheat the sauce in a saucepan if necessary and serve it over pasta or roasted vegetables for a delectable and dairy-free Alfredo experience.

Calories: 150 Protein: 3g Carbohydrates: 4g Dietary Fiber: 2g Sugars: 2g Fat: 12g Saturated Fat: 1.5g

Tomato Basil Bruschetta:

Ingredients:
- 4 ripe tomatoes, diced
- 1/4 cup fresh basil leaves, chopped
- 2 garlic cloves, minced
- 2 tablespoons balsamic vinegar
- 2 tablespoons extra-virgin olive oil
- Salt and pepper to taste
- Baguette slices, toasted

Instructions:
1. In a bowl, combine diced tomatoes, chopped basil, minced garlic, balsamic vinegar, extra-virgin olive oil, salt, and pepper. Mix well.
2. Allow the bruschetta mixture to marinate for at least 15 minutes to let the flavors meld together.

3. Serve the tomato basil bruschetta on toasted baguette slices for a delicious appetizer or light snack.

Calories: 100 Protein: 4g Carbohydrates: 15g
Dietary Fiber: 3g Sugars: 4g Fat: 6g

Caprese Salad Skewers:

Ingredients:
- Cherry tomatoes
- Fresh mozzarella balls
- Fresh basil leaves
- Balsamic glaze
- Wooden skewers

Instructions:
1. Thread cherry tomatoes, fresh mozzarella balls, and fresh basil leaves onto wooden skewers in alternating order.
2. Arrange the caprese salad skewers on a serving platter.
3. Drizzle balsamic glaze over the skewers for a burst of flavor and visual appeal.
4. Serve these delightful caprese salad skewers as a refreshing and elegant appetizer.

Calories: 50 Protein: 3g Carbohydrates: 4g Dietary
Fiber: 1g Sugars: 2g Fat: 5g

Zucchini Fritters with Yogurt Sauce:

Ingredients:
- 2 large zucchinis, grated and squeezed to remove excess moisture
- 1/2 cup all-purpose flour (or almond flour for a gluten-free option)
- 1/4 cup grated Parmesan cheese (or nutritional yeast for a dairy-free option)
- 1 garlic clove, minced
- 2 green onions, thinly sliced
- 1/4 cup chopped fresh parsley
- 1/4 cup chopped fresh dill
- 2 large eggs, lightly beaten
- Salt and pepper to taste
- Olive oil for frying

Yogurt Sauce:
- 1 cup Greek yogurt (or coconut yogurt for a dairy-free option)
- 1 tablespoon lemon juice
- 1 tablespoon chopped fresh dill
- Salt and pepper to taste

Instructions:
1. In a large bowl, combine grated zucchinis, all-purpose flour, grated Parmesan cheese, minced garlic, sliced green onions, chopped parsley, chopped dill, and lightly beaten eggs. Mix well.
2. Season the mixture with salt and pepper to taste.
3. Heat olive oil in a skillet over medium heat.
4. Drop spoonfuls of the zucchini mixture into the skillet and flatten them slightly to form fritters.
5. Cook the fritters for 2-3 minutes on each side or until they turn golden brown and crispy.
6. In a separate bowl, mix Greek yogurt, lemon juice, chopped dill, salt, and pepper to create the yogurt sauce.
7. Serve the zucchini fritters with the refreshing yogurt sauce for a flavorful and nutritious appetizer.

Calories: 200 Protein: 7g Carbohydrates: 15g
Dietary Fiber: 4g Sugars: 4g Fat: 8g

DRESSING, SAUCES AND SPREADS RECIPES

Roasted Red Pepper Spread:

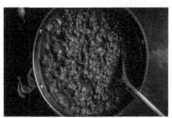

Ingredients:
- 1 cup roasted red peppers (from a jar or homemade)
- 1/2 cup raw walnuts
- 2 tablespoons olive oil
- 1 tablespoon lemon juice
- 1 garlic clove
- 1/2 teaspoon smoked paprika
- Salt and pepper to taste

Instructions:
1. In the Vitamix blender, combine roasted red peppers, raw walnuts, olive oil, lemon juice, garlic, smoked paprika, salt, and pepper.
2. Blend until the spread reaches a smooth and creamy consistency.
3. Enjoy this roasted red pepper spread on sandwiches, wraps, or as a flavorful dip for crackers and bread.

Calories: 50 Protein: 3g Carbohydrates: 5g Dietary Fiber: 3g Sugars: 4g Fat: 8g

Honey Mustard Sauce:

Ingredients:
- 1/4 cup Dijon mustard
- 2 tablespoons honey (or maple syrup for a vegan option)
- 2 tablespoons apple cider vinegar
- 2 tablespoons olive oil
- 1 garlic clove
- Salt and pepper to taste

Instructions:
1. In the Vitamix blender, blend Dijon mustard, honey, apple cider vinegar, olive oil, garlic, salt, and pepper until well combined.
2. Adjust the sweetness and tanginess to your liking by adding more honey or vinegar.
3. Drizzle this delicious honey mustard sauce over salads, grilled chicken, or use it as a dipping sauce for chicken tenders or veggies.

Calories: 60 Protein: 1g Carbohydrates: 5g Dietary Fiber: 0g Sugars: 6g Fat: 8g

Creamy Cashew Spread:

Ingredients:
- 1 cup raw cashews, soaked in water for 2 hours and drained
- 1/4 cup water
- 2 tablespoons nutritional yeast
- 2 tablespoons lemon juice
- 1 garlic clove
- 1/2 teaspoon onion powder
- Salt and pepper to taste

Instructions:
1. In the Vitamix blender, blend soaked cashews, water, nutritional yeast, lemon juice, garlic, onion powder, salt, and pepper until creamy and smooth.
2. Adjust the consistency with more water if needed.
3. This creamy cashew spread is a perfect dairy-free alternative to cream cheese and can be used on bagels, sandwiches, or as a dip for veggie sticks.

Calories: 60 Protein: 3g Carbohydrates: 4g Dietary Fiber: 2g Sugars: 2g Fat: 6g

Lemon Herb Vinaigrette:

Ingredients:
- 1/4 cup lemon juice
- 1/4 cup extra-virgin olive oil
- 1 tablespoon Dijon mustard
- 1 garlic clove
- 1 tablespoon fresh thyme leaves
- 1 tablespoon fresh parsley leaves
- Salt and pepper to taste

Instructions:
1. In the Vitamix blender, combine lemon juice, extra-virgin olive oil, Dijon mustard, garlic, thyme leaves, parsley leaves, salt, and pepper.
2. Blend until all ingredients are well incorporated and the vinaigrette has a smooth consistency.
3. Drizzle this zesty lemon herb vinaigrette over salads, roasted vegetables, or grilled chicken for a burst of flavor.

Calories: 50 Protein: 1g Carbohydrates: 2g Dietary Fiber: 0g Sugars: 1g Fat: 4g

Spicy Sriracha Mayo:

Ingredients:
- 1/4 cup mayonnaise (or vegan mayo)
- 1 tablespoon Sriracha sauce
- 1 tablespoon lime juice
- 1/2 teaspoon garlic powder
- Salt to taste

Instructions:
1. In the Vitamix blender, combine mayonnaise, Sriracha sauce, lime juice, garlic powder, and a pinch of salt.
2. Blend until the sauce is well mixed and has a smooth texture.
3. Use this spicy Sriracha mayo to add a kick to your burgers, sandwiches, or as a dipping sauce for fries and chicken tenders.

Calories: 50 Protein: 1g Carbohydrates: 3g Dietary Fiber: 0g Sugars: 1g Fat: 8g

Tangy Tzatziki Sauce:

Ingredients:
- 1 cup Greek yogurt (or coconut yogurt for a dairy-free option)
- 1/2 cucumber, grated and drained
- 2 tablespoons fresh dill
- 1 tablespoon lemon juice
- 1 garlic clove
- 1 tablespoon extra-virgin olive oil
- Salt and pepper to taste

Instructions:
1. In the Vitamix blender, blend Greek yogurt, grated cucumber, fresh dill, lemon juice, garlic, extra-virgin olive oil, salt, and pepper until the sauce is well combined.
2. Adjust the consistency with a splash of water if needed.
3. Serve this tangy tzatziki sauce with grilled meats, falafels, or as a refreshing dip for pita bread and veggies.

Calories: 30 Protein: 2g Carbohydrates: 5g Dietary Fiber: 2g Sugars: 3g Fat: 4g

Spicy Guacamole

Ingredients:
- 2 ripe avocados, peeled and pitted
- 1/4 cup diced tomatoes
- 1/4 cup diced red onion
- 1 jalapeño, seeds removed and finely chopped
- 2 tablespoons chopped fresh cilantro
- 1 tablespoon lime juice
- Salt and pepper to taste

Instructions:
1. In the Vitamix blender, blend ripe avocados until creamy.
2. Transfer the blended avocados to a bowl and fold in diced tomatoes, diced red onion, jalapeño, chopped cilantro, lime juice, salt, and pepper.
3. Mix well until all ingredients are evenly distributed, leaving some chunky texture for a perfect guacamole.
4. Serve this spicy guacamole with tortilla chips, tacos, or as a topping for grilled meats.

Calories: 50g Protein: 2g Carbohydrates: 4g Dietary Fiber: 4g Sugars: 2g Fat: 7g

Chunky Salsa:

Ingredients:
- 1 can (14.5 oz) diced tomatoes, drained
- 1/4 cup chopped red onion
- 1/4 cup chopped fresh cilantro
- 1 jalapeño, seeds removed and finely chopped
- 1 garlic clove
- 1 tablespoon lime juice
- Salt and pepper to taste

Instructions:
1. In the Vitamix blender, pulse the drained diced tomatoes, red onion, cilantro, jalapeño, garlic, and lime juice a few times until you achieve a chunky texture.
2. Season the salsa with salt and pepper to taste.
3. Serve this flavorful chunky salsa with tortilla chips, as a topping for tacos, or with grilled chicken and fish.

Calories: 25g Protein: 1g Carbohydrates: 4g Dietary Fiber: 2g Sugars: 3g Fat: 1g

DESSERTS RECIPES

Creamy Chocolate Avocado Pudding:

Ingredients:
- 2 ripe avocados
- 1/4 cup cocoa powder
- 1/4 cup honey or maple syrup
- 1/4 cup almond milk
- 1 tsp vanilla extract
- Pinch of salt

Instructions:
1. Scoop out the flesh of the avocados and add them to the Vitamix blender.
2. Add cocoa powder, honey (or maple syrup), almond milk, vanilla extract, and a pinch of salt.
3. Blend until smooth and creamy.
4. Transfer the pudding to serving dishes and refrigerate for at least 30 minutes before serving.

Calories: 250 Protein: 3g Carbohydrates: 15g
Dietary Fiber: 5g Sugars: 8g Fat: 15g

Mixed Berry Sorbet:

Ingredients:
- 2 cups mixed berries (strawberries, blueberries, raspberries)
- 1/4 cup honey or agave syrup
- 1 tbsp lemon juice

Instructions:
1. Add the mixed berries, honey (or agave syrup), and lemon juice to the Vitamix blender.
2. Blend until smooth and well combined.
3. Pour the mixture into a shallow container and freeze for 2-3 hours, stirring every 30 minutes to break up any ice crystals.
4. Once frozen, scoop the sorbet into serving bowls and garnish with fresh berries.

Calories: 250 Protein: 1g Carbohydrates: 25g
Dietary Fiber: 4g Sugars: 20g Fat: 1g

Peanut Butter Banana Nice Cream

Ingredients:
- 2 ripe bananas, frozen
- 1/4 cup creamy peanut butter
- 1/4 cup almond milk
- 1 tbsp honey or maple syrup (optional)

Instructions:
1. Place the frozen bananas, peanut butter, almond milk, and honey (or maple syrup) in the Vitamix blender.
2. Blend until smooth and creamy.
3. Transfer the nice cream to a freezer-safe container and freeze for 1-2 hours to firm up.
4. Serve in bowls or cones and enjoy this guilt-free treat.

Calories: 300 Protein: 10g Carbohydrates: 30g Dietary Fiber: 3g Sugars: 15g Fat: 10g

Coconut Mango Chia Pudding:

Ingredients:
- 1 cup coconut milk
- 1 ripe mango, diced
- 2 tbsp chia seeds
- 1 tbsp honey or agave syrup
- Shredded coconut and fresh mango slices for garnish

Instructions:
1. Add the coconut milk, diced mango, chia seeds, and honey (or agave syrup) to the Vitamix blender.
2. Blend until the mixture is smooth and creamy.
3. Pour the pudding into individual jars or glasses.
4. Cover and refrigerate for at least 4 hours or overnight to let the chia seeds plump up.
5. Garnish with shredded coconut and fresh mango slices before serving.

Calories: 150 Protein: 4g Carbohydrates: 25g
Dietary Fiber: 5g Sugars: 15g Fat: 8g

Vanilla Almond Milkshake

Ingredients:
- 2 cups vanilla ice cream
- 1 cup almond milk
- 1 tsp vanilla extract
- 2 tbsp almond butter
- Whipped cream and sliced almonds for topping (optional)

Instructions:
1. In the Vitamix blender, combine vanilla ice cream, almond milk, vanilla extract, and almond butter.
2. Blend until smooth and creamy.
3. Pour the milkshake into glasses and top with whipped cream and sliced almonds if desired.

Calories: 250 Protein: 7g Carbohydrates: 25g
Dietary Fiber: 3g Sugars: 15g Fat: 10g

Creamy Mango Sorbet:

Ingredients:
- 2 cups frozen mango chunks
- 1/4 cup coconut milk
- 2 tbsp honey or maple syrup
- 1 tsp lime juice

Instructions:
1. Add frozen mango, coconut milk, honey (or maple syrup), and lime juice to the Vitamix blender.
2. Start on low speed and gradually increase to high until the mixture is smooth and creamy.
3. Transfer the sorbet into a container and freeze for at least 1 hour before serving. Enjoy!

Calories: 150 Protein: 1g Carbohydrates: 25g
Dietary Fiber: 4g Sugars: 20g Fat: 1g

Chocolate Avocado Pudding:

Ingredients:
- 2 ripe avocados, peeled and pitted
- 1/4 cup cocoa powder
- 1/4 cup honey or agave syrup
- 1/4 cup almond milk
- 1 tsp vanilla extract

Instructions:
1. Place the avocados, cocoa powder, honey (or agave syrup), almond milk, and vanilla extract in the Vitamix blender.
2. Blend on high speed until the mixture is smooth and creamy.
3. Refrigerate the pudding for at least 30 minutes before serving. Top with fresh berries if desired.

Calories: 250 Protein: 3g Carbohydrates: 15g
Dietary Fiber: 5g Sugars: 8g Fat: 15g

Strawberry Banana Nice Cream:

Ingredients:
- 2 cups frozen strawberries
- 2 ripe bananas
- 1/4 cup Greek yogurt
- 2 tbsp honey or maple syrup

Instructions:
1. Combine frozen strawberries, ripe bananas, Greek yogurt, and honey (or maple syrup) in the Vitamix blender.
2. Blend on high speed until the mixture turns into a creamy ice cream-like texture.
3. Serve immediately as a guilt-free treat or freeze for a firmer texture.

Calories: 150 Protein: 3g Carbohydrates: 25g Dietary Fiber: 5g Sugars: 20g Fat: 2g

Pineapple Coconut Smoothie Bowl:

Ingredients:
- 1 cup frozen pineapple chunks
- 1/2 cup coconut milk
- 1 ripe banana
- 1/4 cup Greek yogurt
- Toppings: sliced kiwi, shredded coconut, chia seeds, and granola

Instructions:
1. Combine frozen pineapple, coconut milk, ripe banana, and Greek yogurt in the Vitamix blender.
2. Blend on high until smooth and creamy.
3. Pour the smoothie into a bowl and top with sliced kiwi, shredded coconut, chia seeds, and granola.

Calories: 200 Protein: 10g Carbohydrates: 30g
Dietary Fiber: 4g Sugars: 15g Fat: 8g

Raspberry Lemon Cheesecake Smoothie:

Ingredients:
- 1 cup frozen raspberries
- 1/2 cup plain Greek yogurt
- 1/4 cup cream cheese
- 1 tbsp honey or agave syrup
- 1 tsp lemon zest
- 1/2 cup almond milk

Instructions:
1. Add frozen raspberries, Greek yogurt, cream cheese, honey (or agave syrup), lemon zest, and almond milk to the Vitamix blender.
2. Blend on high speed until smooth and creamy.
3. Pour the smoothie into a glass and garnish with a few fresh raspberries.

Calories: 250 Protein: 10g Carbohydrates: 35g
Dietary Fiber: 4g Sugars: 15g Fat: 8g

Vegan Chocolate Mousse:

Ingredients:
- 1 ripe avocado, peeled and pitted
- 1/4 cup cocoa powder
- 1/4 cup almond milk
- 2 tbsp maple syrup
- 1 tsp vanilla extract

Instructions:
1. Combine the ripe avocado, cocoa powder, almond milk, maple syrup, and vanilla extract in the Vitamix blender.
2. Blend on high speed until the mixture is silky and smooth.
3. Transfer the chocolate mousse into individual serving cups and refrigerate for 30 minutes before enjoying.

Calories: 250 Protein: 4g Carbohydrates: 25g
Dietary Fiber: 5g Sugars: 15g Fat: 10g

Blueberry Almond Butter Smoothie:

Ingredients:
- 1 cup fresh or frozen blueberries
- 2 tbsp almond butter
- 1 ripe banana
- 1 cup almond milk
- 1 tsp honey or agave syrup (optional, for added sweetness)

Instructions:
1. Place the blueberries, almond butter, ripe banana, almond milk, and honey (or agave syrup) in the Vitamix blender.
2. Blend on high speed until all ingredients are well combined.
3. Pour the smoothie into a glass and enjoy this delicious and nutritious treat.

Calories: 250 Protein: 10g Carbohydrates: 25g
Dietary Fiber: 8g Sugars: 10g Fat: 12g

JUICE AND SMOOTHIES

Tropical Paradise Smoothie:

Ingredients:
- 1 cup fresh pineapple chunks
- 1 ripe banana
- 1/2 cup coconut milk
- 1/2 cup orange juice
- 1 tbsp chia seeds (optional, for added nutrition)

Instructions:
1. Combine the fresh pineapple chunks, ripe banana, coconut milk, orange juice, and chia seeds (if using) in the Vitamix blender.
2. Blend on high speed until smooth and creamy.
3. Pour the smoothie into a glass, garnish with a pineapple slice, and enjoy the taste of the tropics.

Calories: 200 Protein: 3g Carbohydrates: 35g
Dietary Fiber: 5g Sugars: 25g Fat: 2g

Berry Blast Juice:

Ingredients:
- 1 cup mixed berries (strawberries, blueberries, raspberries)
- 1 apple, cored and sliced
- 1/2 cup water
- 1 tsp honey or agave syrup (optional, for added sweetness)

Instructions:
1. Add the mixed berries, apple slices, water, and honey (or agave syrup) to the Vitamix blender.
2. Blend on high speed until the juice is well mixed and smooth.
3. Pour the berry blast juice into a glass, and savor the burst of berry flavors.

Calories: 250 Protein: 2g Carbohydrates: 25g
Dietary Fiber: 5g Sugars: 15g Fat: 2g

Green Detox Juice:

Ingredients:
- 1 cucumber, peeled and chopped
- 2 cups fresh spinach leaves
- 1 green apple, cored and sliced
- 1/2 lemon, peeled
- 1-inch piece of ginger, peeled

Instructions:
1. Place the cucumber, fresh spinach leaves, green apple slices, lemon, and ginger in the Vitamix blender.
2. Blend on high speed until the juice is thoroughly blended.
3. Pour the green detox juice into a glass, and feel refreshed and revitalized.

Calories: 70 Protein: 2g Carbohydrates: 15g Dietary Fiber: 4g Sugars: 8g Fat: 1g

Creamy Banana Oat Smoothie

Ingredients:
- 2 ripe bananas
- 1/2 cup rolled oats
- 1 cup almond milk
- 1 tbsp almond butter
- 1 tsp honey or maple syrup (optional, for added sweetness)

Instructions:
1. Combine the ripe bananas, rolled oats, almond milk, almond butter, and honey (or maple syrup) in the Vitamix blender.
2. Blend on high speed until the smoothie is creamy and velvety.
3. Pour the creamy banana oat smoothie into a glass, and enjoy the delightful taste and texture.

Calories: 300 Protein: 4g Carbohydrates: 25g
Dietary Fiber: 4g Sugars: 25g Fat: 8g

Citrus Sunshine Juice:

Ingredients:
- 2 oranges, peeled and segmented
- 1 grapefruit, peeled and segmented
- 1 lemon, peeled
- 1-inch piece of turmeric root (or 1/2 tsp ground turmeric)
- 1/2 cup water

Instructions:
1. Add the oranges, grapefruit, lemon, turmeric root, and water to the Vitamix blender.
2. Blend on high speed until the juice is well blended and vibrant.
3. Pour the citrus sunshine juice into a glass, and start your day with a burst of citrus goodness.

Calories: 60 Protein: 2g Carbohydrates: 15g Dietary Fiber: 4g Sugars: 8g Fat: 1g

Energizing Green Juice:

Ingredients:
- 2 cups kale leaves
- 1 green apple, cored and sliced
- 1 cucumber, peeled and chopped
- 1 lemon, peeled
- 1-inch piece of ginger, peeled

Instructions:
1. Place the kale leaves, green apple slices, cucumber, lemon, and ginger in the Vitamix blender.
2. Blend on high speed until the juice is vibrant and well combined.
3. Pour the energizing green juice into a glass, and feel rejuvenated and ready to take on the day.

Calories: 70 Protein: 2g Carbohydrates: 20g Dietary Fiber: 4g Sugars: 10g Fat: 1g

Piña Colada Smoothie:

Ingredients:
- 1 cup fresh pineapple chunks
- 1/2 ripe banana
- 1/2 cup coconut milk
- 1/2 cup pineapple juice
- 1/4 cup plain Greek yogurt

Instructions:
1. Add the fresh pineapple chunks, ripe banana, coconut milk, pineapple juice, and Greek yogurt to the Vitamix blender.
2. Blend on high speed until the smoothie is creamy and tropical.
3. Pour the piña colada smoothie into a glass, and transport yourself to a sunny island getaway.

Calories: 250 Protein: 3g Carbohydrates: 25g
Dietary Fiber: 4g Sugars: 25g Fat: 8g

Immunity Booster Juice:

Ingredients:
- 2 oranges, peeled and segmented
- 1 lemon, peeled
- 1-inch piece of fresh turmeric root (or 1/2 tsp ground turmeric)
- 1-inch piece of fresh ginger, peeled
- 1 carrot, peeled and chopped
- 1/2 cup water

Instructions:
1. Combine the oranges, lemon, turmeric root, ginger, carrot, and water in the Vitamix blender.
2. Blend on high speed until the juice is smooth and packed with immunity-boosting nutrients.
3. Pour the immunity booster juice into a glass, and support your well-being with this nourishing elixir.

Calories: 50 Protein: 2g Carbohydrates: 15g Dietary Fiber: 4g Sugars: 8g Fat: 1g

Carrot Ginger Turmeric Juice:

Ingredients:
- 4 large carrots, peeled and chopped
- 1-inch piece of fresh ginger, peeled
- 1-inch piece of fresh turmeric root (or 1/2 tsp ground turmeric)
- 1 orange, peeled and segmented
- 1/2 cup water

Instructions:
1. Add the carrots, ginger, turmeric root, orange segments, and water to the Vitamix blender.
2. Blend on high speed until the juice is vibrant and brimming with immune-boosting properties.
3. Pour the carrot ginger turmeric juice into a glass, and let its golden hue brighten your day.

Calories: 80 Protein: 2g Carbohydrates: 15g Dietary Fiber: 2g Sugars: 10g Fat: 1g

BABY FOOD RECIPES

Creamy Avocado Banana Puree

Ingredients:
- 1 ripe avocado, peeled and pitted
- 1 ripe banana
- 2-3 tbsp breast milk or formula (for desired consistency)

Instructions:
1. Add the ripe avocado and banana to the Vitamix blender.
2. Blend on low speed, gradually increasing to high, until the mixture is smooth and creamy.
3. If needed, add breast milk or formula to achieve the desired consistency.
4. Transfer the creamy avocado banana puree to a baby food container and serve.

Calories: 100 Protein: 2g Carbohydrates: 8g Dietary Fiber: 4g Sugars: 4g Fat: 7g

Sweet Potato and Apple Mash

Ingredients:
- 1 small sweet potato, peeled and chopped
- 1 sweet apple, cored and chopped
- 2-3 tbsp water or homemade vegetable broth (for cooking)

Instructions:
1. Steam the sweet potato and apple until soft and tender.
2. Add the steamed sweet potato and apple to the Vitamix blender along with a little water or homemade vegetable broth for easier blending.
3. Blend on low speed, gradually increasing to high, until the mixture forms a smooth and velvety mash.
4. Allow the sweet potato and apple mash to cool before serving.

Calories: 150 Protein: 2g Carbohydrates: 25g
Dietary Fiber: 4g Sugars: 10g Fat: 1g

Spinach and Pear Puree:

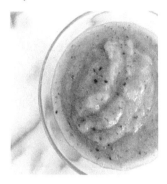

Ingredients:
- 1 cup fresh spinach leaves
- 1 ripe pear, peeled, cored, and chopped
- 2-3 tbsp water or homemade vegetable broth (for cooking)

Instructions:
1. Steam the fresh spinach leaves and chopped pear until tender.
2. Add the steamed spinach and pear to the Vitamix blender along with a little water or homemade vegetable broth for easier blending.
3. Blend on low speed, gradually increasing to high, until the mixture turns into a smooth and vibrant green puree.
4. Allow the spinach and pear puree to cool before serving.

Calories: 80 Protein: 2g Carbohydrates: 15g Dietary Fiber: 5g Sugars: 8g Fat: 1g

Carrot and Lentil Mash

Ingredients:
- 1 large carrot, peeled and chopped
- 1/4 cup cooked lentils
- 2-3 tbsp water or homemade vegetable broth (for cooking)

Instructions:
1. Steam the chopped carrot until soft.
2. Add the steamed carrot and cooked lentils to the Vitamix blender along with a little water or homemade vegetable broth for easier blending.
3. Blend on low speed, gradually increasing to high, until the mixture forms a smooth and nutritious mash.
4. Allow the carrot and lentil mash to cool before serving.

Calories: 100 Protein: 4g Carbohydrates: 25g
Dietary Fiber: 7g Sugars: 6g Fat: 2g

Butternut Squash and Apple Puree

Ingredients:
- 1 cup butternut squash, peeled and diced
- 1 sweet apple, peeled, cored, and chopped
- 2-3 tbsp water or homemade vegetable broth (for cooking)

Instructions:
1. Steam the diced butternut squash and chopped apple until soft.
2. Add the steamed butternut squash and apple to the Vitamix blender along with a little water or homemade vegetable broth for easier blending.
3. Blend on low speed, gradually increasing to high, until the mixture forms a smooth and velvety puree.
4. Allow the butternut squash and apple puree to cool before serving.

Calories: 100 Protein: 2g Carbohydrates: 25g
Dietary Fiber: 5g Sugars: 10g Fat: 1g

Green Pea and Mint Mash:

Ingredients:
- 1 cup cooked green peas
- 1-2 sprigs fresh mint leaves
- 2-3 tbsp water or homemade vegetable broth (for blending)

Instructions:
1. Cook green peas according to package instructions and let them cool.
2. Rinse and pat dry fresh mint leaves.
3. Add the cooked green peas and fresh mint leaves to the Vitamix blender along with a little water or homemade vegetable broth for easier blending.
4. Blend on low speed, gradually increasing to high, until the mixture forms a smooth and flavorful mash.
5. Allow the green pea and mint mash to cool before serving.

Calories: 150 Protein: 4g Carbohydrates: 15g
Dietary Fiber: 5g Sugars: 5g Fat: 4g

CONCLUSION

In conclusion, "The Complete Vitamix Blender Cookbook 2023: Transform Your Health With 500 Smoothies, Soups, Side Dishes, Nut Butters, Ice Cream, Appetizers, Cookies, Cakes And Baking, Entrees, Breads, Baby Food" is a labor of love, crafted to inspire and empower you to make the most of your Vitamix blender. From wholesome breakfasts to mouthwatering desserts, this cookbook offers a diverse array of recipes that cater to every palate and dietary preference.

As I reflect on the countless hours spent perfecting these recipes, my heart swells with excitement to share them with you. I genuinely believe that incorporating the power of the Vitamix blender into your culinary journey will elevate your cooking experience to new heights.

Your positive reviews and feedback are what keep authors like me motivated to create more meaningful content. If these recipes have brought joy to your kitchen and enriched your dining experiences, I humbly request that you take a moment to leave a review on Amazon. Your heartfelt comments will not only brighten my day but also inspire other home cooks to explore the endless possibilities of the Vitamix blender.

Thank you for embarking on this flavorful journey with me, and here's to many more delectable meals shared with your loved ones. May your Vitamix blender become your trusted kitchen companion, blending health and happiness in every dish.

Happy blending and bon appétit!

Made in the USA
Las Vegas, NV
13 December 2023

82657191R10056